W9-BDV-092

Fun Things
Milk Jugs to Do with

by Marne Ventura

A+ Books are published by Capstone Press,
1710 Roe Crest Drive, North Mankato, Minnesota 56003
www.capstonepub.com

Library of Congress Cataloging-in-Publication Data
Ventura, Marne.
Fun Things to Do with Milk Jugs / by Marne Ventura.
pages cm—(A+ Books. 10 Things to Do)
Includes bibliographical references.
Summary: "Full-color photos and simple, step-by-step instructions describe 10 crafts and activities
using empty milk jugs and common materials found around the house"—Provided by publisher.
Audience: Grades K–3.
ISBN 978-1-4765-9894-9 (library binding)
ISBN 978-1-4765-9898-7 (ebook pdf)
1. Plastics craft—Juvenile literature. 2. Plastic bottle craft—Juvenile literature. 3. Recycling
(Waste, etc.)—Juvenile literature. I. Title.
TT297.V45 2015
745.57'2—dc23   2014018252

Editorial Credits
Jeni Wittrock, editor; Bobbie Nuytten, designer; Sarah Schuette, photo stylist; Marcy Morin,
studio scheduler; Kim Braun, project production; Tori Abraham, production specialist

Photo Credits
Images by Capstone Studio: Karon Dubke except Shutterstock: Accent, 26 (background),
Ambient Ideas, 14 (top), Andy Lidstone, 12 (t), blue hand, 28 (fish), 30 (fish),
D. Kucharski K. Kucharska, 8 (t), ScottChan, 28 (bubbles), 30 (bubbles)

Printed in the United States of America in
North Mankato, Minnesota
032014   008087CGF14

Table of Contents

Introduction

Have an empty milk jug? Why not wash it up and put it to good use? All the projects in this book reuse a gallon or half-gallon plastic milk jug. Add a few basic tools and simple materials, and, voilà! You'll have something new!

Many of the supplies needed to complete these projects are items you might already have in your home. If not, you can find what you need at dollar stores, discount department stores, and craft shops.

Have a blast reusing materials and making the projects in this book. Then use your imagination to come up with even more ways to reuse things you find!

Memory Game with Piece Keeper

Supplies

- » 1 half-gallon milk jug
- » 16 identical milk jug lids
- » 16 identical stickers
- » 8 different pairs of identical stickers
- » scissors
- » hole punch
- » permanent markers
- » ribbon, yarn, or string
- » stickers for decorating the piece keeper

 Stick one of the 16 identical stickers to the top of each lid.

 Stick one of the 8 pairs of identical stickers inside each lid.

 Ask an adult to cut a curved flap on one flat side of the jug.

 Use the hole punch to make a hole just above the flap. Punch a second hole in the center of the top of the flap.

Lace the ribbon through the two punched-out holes. Tie the ribbon when game pieces are being stored inside. Untie the ribbon and open the flap to take the pieces out and play.

 Decorate the jug with extra stickers or with markers.

Play Memory Match Up: Lay the lids, right-side up, in a 4-by-4 grid. With a friend, take turns flipping over two lids at a time. If you get a match, take the lids. If not, turn them back over. The player with the most matches wins. Use the milk jug to store the game.

Mini Garden

Supplies

» 1 gallon milk jug
» scissors
» permanent markers
» pushpin
» potting soil
» 3–4 flower seeds
» ribbon
» plastic plate

1 Ask an adult to cut an opening in the milk jug, as shown. Do not remove the side with the handle, which makes the garden easy to carry. Use permanent markers to decorate the jug.

2 Use the pushpin to poke 20 holes in the bottom of the jug for drainage.

3 Fill your jug with potting soil.

4 Plant three or four seeds. Leave plenty of space between the seeds.

5 Add a final touch by tying a ribbon around the jug's lid.

6 Place the planter in a warm, sunny window. Put a plate beneath the planter to catch any water that drains out. Or put the planter outside.

9

Ball Toss

Supplies

» 1 gallon or half-gallon milk jug with lid
» scissors
» white glue
» wide ribbon
» thin ribbon
» button
» yarn or string
» yarn pom-pom or small Wiffle ball

1. Ask an adult to cut off the base of the jug. Recycle the base or save it for another project.

2. Glue the wide ribbon around the cut edge of the jug. Glue the thin ribbon along the center of the wide ribbon. Glue a button in the center of the ribbon for decoration.

3. Remove the lid. Thread the string through the opening so that about 2 feet (0.6 meter) hang out.

4. Screw the lid back on to hold the string in place.

5. Tie the end of the string to the pom-pom or ball.

Toss the Ball: Hold the jug by the handle with the open base facing upward. Swing the jug so the pom-pom flies up. Try to catch the pom-pom in the jug.

Sailboat

Supplies

» 1 half-gallon milk jug with lid
» scissors
» acrylic paint
» paintbrush
» 12 inch (30.5 centimeter) wooden dowel
» scrapbook paper or craft paper
» white glue
» stickers

1 Have an adult cut a rectangle from the side of the milk carton with the handle.

2 Paint your boat and let it dry.

3 Cut a hole between the rectangle and the handle. Stick the dowel into the hole and push it down to the bottom of the jug.

4 Decorate the boat with craft paper and stickers.

5 Glue triangle sails back-to-back with one side glued along the dowel.

Float a Boat: Put the cap on the jug. Use decoupage or ModPodge to make the bottom waterproof.

Piggy Bank

Supplies

- » 1 gallon milk jug with lid
- » 2 cardboard tubes
- » scissors
- » white glue
- » acrylic paint
- » paintbrush
- » big stick-on wiggly eyes
- » 2 white milk jug lids
- » black marker
- » 2 felt triangles
- » black marker
- » chenille stem

 1 Cut two cardboard tubes in half. These are the pig's legs. Glue them to the side of the milk jug opposite the handle.

 2 Paint the pig and let it dry.

 3 Stick one eye on each milk jug lid. Glue the lids on either side of the jug's handle.

 4 Glue felt triangles on the jug for ears. Draw nostrils on the cap with the black marker.

5 Poke a hole near the top of the back. Stick the chenille stem in halfway. Curl it around your finger to make the tail.

6 Ask an adult to use a scissors to cut a coin slot on the top side.

Save Your Money: Drop coins into your piggy bank. Keep track of your savings by writing the amounts in a notebook. When you are ready to spend your money, take off the nose lid and pour it out.

Plastic Bag Monster

Supplies

» 1 gallon milk jug
» utility knife
» scissors
» acrylic paint
» paintbrush
» stick-on wiggly eyes
» craft paper
» white glue
» plastic grocery bags
» pom-pom (optional)
» felt bow (optional)

1. Ask an adult to use the utility knife and scissors to cut a wide mouth on the side of the milk jug that is opposite the handle.

2. Paint the jug and let it dry.

3. Stick on the eyes above the center of the mouth.

4. Cut two arms and hair from craft paper. Glue the arms to the sides of the jug. Glue the hair on top.

5. Use craft paper or other supplies to add teeth, a nose, and other features. A pom-pom and felt bow are cute additions.

Recycle Plastic Grocery Bags:
Fill your monster's mouth with plastic grocery bags. Keep her in the car or kitchen. Reuse the bags to hold trash, lunches, or groceries.

Hungry Frogs

Supplies

» 3 gallon milk jugs
» utility knife
» scissors
» green acrylic paint
» paintbrush
» stick-on wiggly eyes
» permanent markers
» green felt
» pink felt
» 3 small socks
» 3 chenille stems

1 Ask an adult use the utility knife and scissors to cut out a rounded mouth on each jug.

2 Paint the jugs green.

3 Stick two eyes to each jug.

4 Cut six arms and six legs from green felt. Glue two hands and two feet to the sides of each jug.

5 Cut three tongues from the pink felt. Glue the tongues inside the frogs' mouths.

6 Make bugs to feed the frogs! Fold each sock into a tiny ball. Twist a chenille stem around each sock. Curl the ends to make antennas. Finally, add two wiggly eyes to each sock.

Feed the Frogs: Line up the frogs on the ground. Stand back a few feet. Now throw the bugs, one at a time, into the frogs' mouths. Can you get one bug into each mouth? Can you get three bugs into one frog's mouth? TIP: If the frogs fall over easily, anchor them by putting sand or small rocks inside them.

Bird Feeder

Supplies

- 1 half-gallon milk jug with lid
- utility knife
- scissors
- hole punch
- thin dowel at least 1 foot (30 cm) long
- acrylic paints
- paintbrush
- permanent black marker
- plastic liner from box of cereal
- glue gun
- bits of bark, dry leaves, or twigs
- sturdy stick
- yarn or twine
- wooden craft sticks
- birdseed

1 Ask an adult to cut circles in two opposite sides of a jug.

2 Use a hole punch to make a hole below the center of each circle. Push the dowel through both holes.

3 Paint the jug and dowel any color you like. When dry, draw a blue circle on one side to look like a window.

4 Cut a 2-inch (5-cm) circle from the plastic cereal-box liner. Cut a slit from the edge to the center. Overlap the slit edges to make a cone shape for the roof.

5 Place the cone on top of the jug opening. Screw on the lid to hold the cone in place.

6 Ask an adult to help you decorate your bird feeder roof. With a hot glue gun, glue bits of bark, twigs, or dry leaves to the cereal liner.

7 Ask an adult to hot glue a sturdy stick across the top of the feeder. Tie yarn or twine to the stick so you can hang the feeder.

8 Add a "Welcome" sign made from wooden craft sticks. Ask an adult to help you hot glue it over one of the doors.

Feed the Birds: Fill the bottom of the jug with birdseed. Hang your feeder in a tree. Sit quietly and watch for birds to come!

Hobby Horse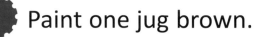

Supplies

- » 2 gallon milk jugs
- » brown acrylic paint
- » paintbrush
- » thick wooden dowel
- » scissors
- » craft glue
- » cardboard
- » markers
- » gold or brown yarn
- » twine or rope
- » ribbon, decorations
- » bandana

1 Paint one jug brown.

2 Ask an adult to cut off the spout of the jug and slice the handle as shown. The dowel should fit into jug, as shown.

3 Paint the dowel brown and let it dry. Glue dowel into place in milk jug.

4 Cut ears from the flat sides of the unpainted milk jug. When dry, glue the ears to the jug.

5 Use cardboard and markers to make the horse's eyes. Glue the eyes to the jug.

Go for a Ride: Pretend to ride your horse by straddling the dowel and holding the neck. Can you trot, gallop, and canter?

 6 Cut pieces of yarn or frayed twine to make the horse's mane. Glue the mane to the jug and dowel, starting between the ears and going down the horse's back. Glue a few more pieces between the ears so it falls into the horse's face.

7 Ask an adult to help you make a bridle with reins for your horse. Use twine, rope, or ribbons. Add a few decorations.

8 Tie a bandana around the dowel just below the jug. Now you're ready to ride!

Aquarium

Supplies

» 2 gallon milk jugs
» utility knife
» scissors
» blue acrylic paint
» paintbrush
» permanent markers: black, orange, red, pink, green, and yellow
» clear tape
» 4 pieces of blue craft wire or chenille stem
» sand
» 3 small rocks or shells
» 4 green chenille stems

1 Ask an adult to cut away two sides of one jug, including the side with the handle. Then ask the adult to cut 4 small slits, evenly spaced, around the top.

2 Paint the aquarium blue.

3 Ask an adult to cut the second jug into flat sections. On these, use markers to draw and color four fish and a starfish. Cut them out.

4 Tape a fish to one end of each blue wire. Poke the other end of each wire upward through one of the slits in the jug. Make a loop in the top of the wire to hold it in place.

2

3

4

5 Put sand and a few rocks and shells in the bottom of the aquarium. Add a starfish too.

 6 Cut the green chenille stems in half. Bend these pieces in half to make seaweed. Place the bent end under a rock to secure.

6

Learn about Fish: What is the difference between saltwater and freshwater fish? Look on the Internet, find a book at the library, or visit an aquarium to learn more.

Read More

Hardy, Emma. *Green Crafts for Children: 35 Step-by-Step Projects Using Natural, Recycled, and Found Materials*. London, England: CICO Books, 2008.

LeBaron, Marie. *Make and Takes for Kids: 50 Crafts Throughout the Year.* Hoboken, N.J.: John Wiley & Sons Inc., 2012.

Locke, Sue. *Back-to-School Crafts.* Creative Crafts for Kids. New York: Gareth Stevens Pub., 2010.

Internet Sites

FactHound offers a safe, fun way to find Internet sites related to this book. All of the sites on FactHound have been researched by our staff.

Here's all you do:

Visit *www.facthound.com*

Type in this code: 9781476598949

Super-cool stuff! Check out projects, games and lots more at **www.capstonekids.com**